"*Good Mourning* is inspirational and helpful. . . . Vivian Greene shows how you can use the power of love to enrich your life."
—Ken Keyes, Jr.
Author of *Handbook to Higher Consciousness*

"Out of your own hurt and loss comes a blessing for all of us. Thank you for *Good Mourning,* Vivian Greene. You've given us an opportunity to turn from grief to growth."
—Reverend John Butcher
Universal Church of Christ

"I read this book again and again. A true artist, Vivian Greene paints with words."
James King, Publisher
Seattle Times

"I am touched by the soulful movement of *Good Mourning.* It draws to me the way Rumi does, and names boldly the right to the texture of life's cycles—all as honorable."
—Susan Musumeci, M.A., MFCC
Transpersonal Therapist

"Excerpts from *Good Mourning* have brightened my eulogies. . . . I highly recommend it for those who grieve, and all who love."
—Rabbi Loring Frank
All Peoples Synagogue

Good Mourning

Chuck
 Your Love Story
  and recovery
   from loss
  would so
 inspire other men.
 The song of the sea
  does not end
   at the shore...
  and your song
   will make
    others dance !
 See you soon...
  with Love
 and appreciation
  Vivian

Other Books and Collector Editions

Kisses

Love Pockets

Hello Up There, Would You Listen to a Bear?

Clover

Home to Happyland

Secret Shelves

OursElves

Star

Imagine

World Family

Nature Magic

If I Had A Father

Selected poems from *Good Mourning* are available as art prints with photos by Kathleen T. Carr (*To Honor the Earth*). For information, contact:

Vivian Greene, Inc. • P.O. Box 4700 • Miami Lakes, Florida 33014

MIRRORS • 244 Madison Avenue, Suite 180 • New York, NY 10016

Good Mourning

What death teaches us about life

by Vivian Greene

MIRRORS
REFLECTING
Love, Peace, Purpose & Change

Cover design by Andrea DuFlon
Illustration and book design, Vivian Greene
Production supervisor, Sandra LaRusso
Typesetting by Archetype Typography, Berkeley, California

©1989, 1992, 1997 by Vivian Greene. All rights reserved under
International and Pan American Copyright Conventions.
Printed in the United States of America. No part of this book
may be used or reproduced in any manner whatsoever
without written permission except in the case of brief
quotations embodied in critical articles and reviews.

ISBN 1-881521-00-1

1. Poetry 2. Personal growth 3. Inspirational

MIRRORS · 244 Madison Avenue, Suite 180 · New York, NY 10016

My Love is undying

therefore

so are you

Acknowledgments

For guidance
> I thank God, my starflower, the angels,
>> Ken Wells and Susan Musumeci.

For friendship
> Bill and Helen Melendez, for putting up with my tearful
> times and inviting me into their home and hearts.
> Sparky, who kept me from abandoning *Kisses* and
> reminded me of what is real.
> Tom Johnson and Willard Colston, who brought me
> home when I was beside myself with grief.

For production
> Some writers love computers. I love people:
> Ravi Romano, Erica Rauzin, Dwina Murphy Gibb,
> the Perez family, Alicia Robinson, John Wilson,
> Debbie Eaglebarger, and Carol LaRusso.

For their example
> Yoko Ono and Jacqueline Kennedy Onassis.

For professional direction
> Don Roth, Chuck Gates, Kathleen T. Carr, Jim Levine,
> Jeremy Tarcher, Sky Canyon, Leslie Meredith,
> Charlie Winton, the Bodhi Tree, and Trina Paulus.

For MOM (Miami Operations Manager)
> Jean Leonard,
> whose dedication relieved me of my "busyness," allowing
> me to focus on my heartfelt work.
> I am blessed to have another friend as rare as Toby.

To my shamrock, three divine men:

Toby
You have died
but all that you have written
on the pages of my heart
lives

Jo
Your evolvement through your illness
(diagnosed as terminal and embraced as eternal)
has blessed me with the ability
to share the feelings I've sheltered so long
and escape my long lonely silence

Alan
When your brother, so young, died
I did not know what to say
to you, whom I have known
for lifetimes.
Our friendship, our bond, validates for me
that a soul never dies.
Your compassion, generosity and brotherhood
are the poetry of life.
The desire to express this to you
and to anyone suffering loss
prompted me to publish this book
Thank you for being you.

Contents

Prologue

Intimately
I write
not knowing
who receives
the embrace
of my feelings
yet knowing
as I unburden
my heart
I reaffirm
the love
that unites
us all
Intimately

"And let there be no purpose in friendship save the deepening of the spirit."
—Kahlil Gibran

Introduction

Good Mourning is not about grief. It is about loving.

The power of Love was the real magician that uncovered my illusions and limitations, and spawned these poems. They helped me create a oneness with Toby, and love itself.

Toby was running in a marathon (a great metaphor for his life) when severe chest pains sent him to a doctor. He was diagnosed with lung cancer. It was his first and last doctor visit that I knew of since I had met him. I was a twenty-one-year-old virgin then. In every respect. Throughout the years this man became my everyman in life—the father, the brother, the husband—the guru I never had. He believed in me. And I believed in him. When he learned he had six months to live, he acted like the restaurant had just run out of vanilla.

He did not believe in "death"; he believed in ascension. And he wanted me to "celebrate" when he left his body.

He did not take medication, agonize, or deteriorate. He died at home with his friends and family around him, as beautifully and lovingly as he had lived.

My "celebration" may have appeared successful, like myself, as I carried on promoting my creations on a worldwide tour. But within the year I was in a near-fatal accident, hospitalizing me for five weeks, and crippling me from my normal lifestyle for several years.

Doctors said I had broken ribs, a separated sternum, a disc out of place in my back, and that I could never ride a bike, a horse, or carry anything heavy (including a baby). Something deeper said I had severe depression.
A broken heart.

I felt there was nobody there who knew and loved me anymore—to back me up, to support me. My body drew my awareness to these areas of pain. There were millions of "fans" for the rich and famous and funny Vivian Greene. But where was Toby, who had known and loved me, just for me?

The me he knew wanted to emerge. The "worldly" self began to melt. My power seemed to have vanished. Physically, I could not continue to promote my work. Emotionally, I felt empty, nakedly alone. Financially, the protective house nobody else had been allowed to enter crumbled with an identity which was no longer enough.

I went to a Loving Relationships seminar. The speaker said, "Missing someone is the absence of love." I thought he was an idiot. I did not understand this any more than Toby's wish for me to celebrate, and the phrase haunted me.

I had to deal with the pain. With my own fear of death. With the drama of the relationships in my life. With loving myself.

It meant working through my anger at having someone so young ripped from my life. And losing not only him, but everything material I had built in my life, slaving from a ghetto kid to a millionairess.

It meant going through my fear of abandonment, of being alone, of not being worth loving enough to have this intimacy again.

It meant going through my guilt—my what ifs, the would haves, should haves, and could haves—I had been so busy, so married to my business.

It meant going through my pain to the point where I stepped off the merry-go-round away from my work to do the hardest work, the inner work that my soul, and perhaps his, was now calling me to do. Instead of forty trade shows a year, I embarked on the longest journey, my spiritual path.

As I went through my fears, and learned to live in the moment, the moment changed the separation to oneness. I looked with my heart. Awakened. I saw that the other side of fear is love. It is all we are. I wanted to be like Toby and not perpetuate suffering. Now, I am healthy and fit and able to do everything the doctors said I could never do again. When I could see the wonder of life, death no longer had a hold over me. When I could open my arms to Love, Love embraced me—even more fully, and in so many ways.

We all have to do our own inner work, and make our own choices. I invite you to share my spiritual journey through these first poems of the hundreds this experience has inspired.

You can have the same experience:

Don't ask why; say "thank you."

Know that love never dies.

Risk being passionate in your life.

The spiritual path is the gateway to love. Real love, not merely romantic love. God's love. The love that is beneath all emotion, and feelings fully felt. The celebration.

Be reflective. And when you see your own reflection, may the peace and joy make your mourning good.

Good
Mourning

Good Mourning

Softly the trembling moon leaves us
and the sun and rainbow
say Good Mourning.

For just as night turns to day
our cycle is a
journey back to Love.

The Quest

You
lit the fire
began the quest
set me flying
from love's nest
to eternity

Hushed

I hear his hushed breathing.
He clutches my finger like an infant
Is this the last night I shall turn off this lamp
In his bed where pain and waiting have crawled
under the covers
where sleep and ecstasy used to play
Maybe the whispers of the night
will turn to whispers of angels
I feel so meek beneath the moon
He wants to go, to ascend, he says
Unlike other men, he has no fear
He will die as he lived
Bravely, confident to meet the gods
A precious pain pressured my chest
as though my ribs were broken
by the ache of my love
and the rarest soul I ever knew
hushed.

To Heaven

I am fortunate
and blessed
to have known
a man's love
so completely
so young
I was only thirty-two
when death drew him
to his other world
and I to mine.
His love sufficed me
so on earth
his departure
began my ardent search
within myself
for
heaven.

Our Heart

Your heart and mine
are great lovers
together
regardless of where we are

Alone

Alone
in my lovely home
on the water,
my tears
fall with the rain.

I write
and I believe
in God's infinite plan
yet I pain
not for Toby, or Jo,
or Stephen, whom I didn't really know,
but for myself
the part of me that aches
and dies each time
another I love
suffers the loss
of their love, and themselves.
My mind grasps the transformation,
immortality, nature's metaphors.
Yet the empty places

. . . hurt.

Crossroads

Good mourning
took many years
for me
to understand.

I am thankful
for my wonderful friends
but so far
he
was the only someone
who really
made a difference.

It is true
I understand
far more
than when he lived.
And he lives
for me
and in me
now.

But
I miss his affection
and his touch
and no one else
has meant
so much.

You
speak of the garden
that loves the rain
and appreciate
the rain
as love
and
love
as
freedom.

It makes me sad
and happy
and full
and loved.
Thank you.

Mildred and Jo

I called my friend, Mildred
and she told me her husband,
her partner for forty-two years,
the man she loves
has cancer
and it is terminal.

I know what that feels like
although it took me many years
to feel it
after my best friend
was told he had six months to live
and left, I thought, until I realized
how much he taught me, before, and now,
and that our relationship never left
love cannot die
and only the cancer was terminal.

Look with Your Heart

In your eyes, he looks pale and drawn
but look with your heart
and see the light in his paleness
and the lightness of his being.

As he sheds his earthly weights,
it is us
who will appear small
and misshapen
in the shadow of his wings.

Emergence

Death and Life
are like
the River and the Sea
The same

Like seeds
buried deep within the earth
Billowing flowers
with their depth of knowing
trust their emergence

Whispers

Wishful far-off whispers
touched with tears
from untethered clouds
fall on my
memories
and my dreams.
And your influence
is brought back to life
like a sleepy flower
awakened
by the rain.

He Goes

He goes not into
    emptiness.
But to
    fulfillment.
And though some nights
    be fitful
You rock the cradle
    of his body
to rest, to peace, to sleep
    until his awakening.

Rest

He wants to take a nap
He wants to take a
    moment of rest upon
    the wind
You may flutter
    in the movement
    or be still.
        Be.

Catalyst

He must go now
For he wants to see you
and how can he see clearly
if he is too close
From afar there will be
the great clarity
you so ardently seek
His terminal illness
is your catalyst
    for your own eternal wellness
As you seek the fitness of your body and mind
He seeks his limitless self
    that rides the stars
        to the timelessness of soul

Where

You are a rainbow of brilliant colors
for him, and so many others.
Although he droops now, a flower
withering, and willing to let go.

And where will he go,
but deep within
the earth and you
to nourish you even more.

Giving

*Giving
is
the
highest
expression
of
our
power*

Reflection

Death encourages living
  to the fullest
and acts like the darkness
  to reflect
  the star

Seeds

As you see your partner
wither like a fruit from the vine
you are gazing at yourself
and your concern is fruitless.
For the dying fruit
is a seed, or many,
which will burst into blossom
and new life.

See not death
but Life
unveiling itself.

Dance On

From the portals of the sunset
you'll be reminded of his love
and not of his needs,
for they will have been met
and now, at last, you can dance
together
to the song in your heart
and enchantment of eternity.

Estuary

I see you
growing
in your wisdom
willingness
strength of purpose
agility,
as you spend
less hours
of
conscious time
floating through hours
of partial presence,
as though part of you
prepares the rest
to pour yourself
into the great
sea.

Love, Life

Love and emptiness
Life and death
Day and night
Ebb and flow
The sea flows in and out

Feel

Your capacity
to feel
is
your capacity
to love

Share Your Burdens

Share your burdens
as well as
your strengths
for
they empower you
to feel your
feelings
fully
and open yourself
to all
that you are

Missing Someone

"Missing someone
is the
absence
of love."

I did not understand.

I felt alone
overwhelmed with responsibility
grievously sad
in so much pain.

I recalled happy times
I did my work
I helped another
and I realized when I was loving

I was experiencing
the love
again
that could not die
   unless I let it
and then I understood.

"Missing someone
is the
absence
of love."

Faith

Faith
is beyond
the reach of
Proof
but within
the reach of
Love

Will

It is not
our circumstances
which
create our
discontent
or
contentment.
It
is
us.

The Kiss of Grace

Life kissed him
good morning
and kissed him
good night

God will kiss him
Good morning
and
we can
dawn
in the acceptance
of the grace

Turn

Turn
your
depression
into
action
and
Death
turns back
into
Life

Flowers

Flowers
perish
petal
by
petal
but
like
us
essence
soul
seeds
remain

Let Go

Clinging to sadness
 multiplies
 its effects

Life is a Miracle

Life
is
a
miracle
born
in
time
until
time
leaves
and
eternity
enters

Light

Men die.

Their light
does not.

It asks
that we
radiate
it here
with our
power
of
Love.

Round and Round

Round and Round
Celestial Circles
Life death Life
the moon
the waters
the earth
Round and Round

Let Him Go

Let him go.
Tell your fear to be quiet.
Trust our own dance
for it is not
his rhythm
or yours
but Life's Sound of Creation
which
will move you
in
perfection.

Life's Design

The core of my apple is a five-pointed star
Perhaps like my core

Cells crisscross through honeycomb
with the intricacy, magic and individuality
of snowflakes
Perhaps like my cells

A snail shell spirals like my inner ear
and I can hear the limitless song
of the entire sea
Perhaps like my inner voice
that speaks to the expanse of me

A golden sunburst encircles the center
of the soul of the carrot root
waiting underground
Perhaps like my soul
waiting, unseen, ready . . .

Our bodies emulate the land's curves.
They are the source of each other.

All remind us of the beautiful
design of life, its unity,
and our place within it.

Why be sad when a star
is called back to the heavens?

We Connect

We connect
with one another.

We connect
the inner and outer
cycles.

Seasonal
Celestial
Communal
Creative
Personal
Connections

say
there is no death.

There is power
to change
ourselves, our society, our earth.

The Form

Sometimes the form
makes me
very comfortable

Sometimes
the form
constricts me

Sometimes the form
embraces
me

Sometimes the form
does not
fit me

Sometimes the form
is spirit
and
there is no need
to
conform

Observance

With his death
as with his life
came a gift:

observance

Airplanes crash
Cancer, AIDS, Stress, eat away bodies.
Children are abandoned, starving.
The Everglades burn, rain forests vanish.
Violence and abuse persist.
People we love, young and good, die

. . . bewildering

Yet
I know
I do not know very much.

I can see only a small part
of the world's pattern
and with observance

comes humility
and gratitude
and another gift:

new possibilities.

Why

When winter
murders
all that we
love
we can do
nothing

Why!?!
the child demanded
mouth pursed
tears tucked
visibly
in angry eyes
Why?

And nature
in her sweet time
answered:

Spring

Web

All is interwoven
like a spider's web
Be gentle
You may trap yourself
and others
or break
the finely planned design
Be gentle
wait
feel
and
move
with care

Wonder

Wondering
if we
failed
someone we love
is
excruciating

Loving
them
is
easy

Loving
ourselves
is
forgiving
and without
judgment

Loving conquers
any failure
including
Wondering

For Truth

Every
person
I know
who
has died
had a
quenchless
thirst
for
truth

Every
tear
I
swallow
feeds
me

Knock Knock

Knock
Knock
It
is
love
I
will
visit
you
if
you
will
open
the
door

Our Bond

There is much
I would like to tell you
but
you need to remember
on your own.
It will mean
much more
to you.
Meanwhile,
our friendship,
that which we share
in conversation, art, places
and feelings,
in our ancient bond,
will often
bring you back
to that place
of forgetting and remembering,
to a life
you once had
and gave up

for all you believe in,
all you were
and are.

One

*Death and distance
cannot separate you
for brotherhood
is one*

*Just as
a flower and its fragrance
are one*

*One drop of water
holds the secrets of the universe*

*One atom
the elements of the earth*

*One thought
Brother
brings all his dreams to life*

One With All

Tides of turmoil
wash in new awareness
Perceptions ride the waves
to the highest good
strengthening
and challenging
us
to be
so humble
and so grand
we can only be
One
with all

One with all
is never alone

What

*What I do not
understand
creates fear.*

*What I experience
lives in me.*

*What I experience
gives birth to love.*

Fulfillment

Feel
the pain
the anger
the love

Feel Fully

Fulfillment
is not self-indulgence
Fulfillment
is self-awareness

Fill your cup full
This is the sacred chalice
which holds the secret
of immortality

Beyond

My soul sailed
in the spacious ocean
looking for you
Under the quilts of foam

If I snuggle here
safely close to the shore
the waves nudge me awake
as you once did

I must reach further
beyond where I thought
safety and comfort
were insured
I must reach beyond
my self-imposed limits

The water is peaceful
in the spacious depths
of the ocean and myself
I feel you know

Song of the Sea

The song
of
the sea
does not
end
at the shore

Clouds

The sky
is covered
but
don't you know
the sun
is awake!

Depth

I did not realize
the depth
of our love
until death
separated us.

I did not know
the depth
of myself
until
the depth
of
my love
was
fully
felt.

Together

*We move
in concert
in a shared journey
interdependently
never alone,
at one with another,
and the oneness
is eternal.*

Music

Music
plays
the singer
and instruments
stop
yet the
vibration
remains
and
sometimes
other times
you hum
or sing along
Music is just like
someone
you Love

Open

Depression
is like a flower
shrinking from the rain
that cheers up
and stands tall
when the sun
Love
is visible again

Waves

When the wave
         finds
the shore
         does it die?

The Lawn

The lawn is folded
softly by the curb

Empty suits and empty hats
rectangle around his empty body
in a hollow box.

Something arises
as he is lowered.

And all the emotions,
and all that was never said
softly sink into the ground
to starch the lawn
neatly folded by the curb.

The grass is cleansed
by the rain
cleared by the breeze
supported
by the Mother earth

In our starch search
for truth
we are loved
like the lawn.

Destiny

I am concerned
he will become
emotionally unbuttoned
by the burdens of business
and reminder of death's toll
on his young life again

His father's dream
His family's empire
His lady's
   mother's
   sister's
   wife's
    fears
weigh so heavily
on this young man's compassionate heart

Father dead
Brother dying
Like he
    in another time
    I painfully recall
Yet at last I
    can understand
    acknowledge
    and be thankful
Death weaves
    the Life, and Love
    we experience today

Ages

Long ages
millenniums of time
weave a thick woolen veil
of ignorance, rituals, and custom
over the ears which cannot hear,
the eyes that cannot see,
and the breath of freedom

Wisdom

*I do not go to
the funeral*

I go into prayer

*I do not seek to understand
the reasons for this death,
that is logic*

*I seek wisdom,
that is love . . .*

*for that
is eternal life
which
I share
here
now
and always*

My Father's Shoes

I tried to fill
my father's shoes.
Then I tried to fill
my brother's.
My feet were not big enough.
So I slipped them
into my own
and they no longer fit.
So I took off my shoes
and felt the earth
beneath my swollen feet,
under which my father and my brother
slumbered.
As I stepped forward
the grass happily stood tall.
There was not a trace
of my steps,
just empty shoes
and at last
a full heart.

Rise

So

the Kingdom
the Company

Pushes you to the throne

Are you reigning?

Or shining?

Moon

Moon
when you thread the night
with stars
cloak my lover
with my love
so I may easily
see him

Blanket

Snow-hushed
burial
of life,
are
you
merely
a blanket
for
slumbering
dreams?

Phantom of the Night

Like the phantom of the night
He disappeared and went away
It was not him that I missed
But his faith, which had wavered

Had I misconceived his intention, his spirit?
Was I haunted by a dead man's love,
unable to connect with another?
We create our own reality.
When then, am I recreating?
Love after love. Pain so deep.
Endless tears never drown the sorrow.

I know this pain is not from disappointment in
him.
I have known it too often and too deeply before.
I know it is death's echo.

Why is it here now·—in a new beginning?
On a healthy rose stem amidst beautiful flowers
one bud refuses to blossom.

Is there a part of me that
was buried with my lover?
I think not.
My longing and my loving
stretch through all boundaries

I deserve love. I love. I see.
It is my faith in him, in myself,
which has wavered and deserted me.

What is death?
Only the passing of the soul
out of the house of flesh.
I am the master of my soul and my house.

My doubt and fear
must become
the new phantoms of the night
so that I may cleanse
my empty house
and invite
Love

Mourning Glory

A morning glory
opened its deep purple heart
and drew a little bird from the sky.
It seemed
neither the flower nor the swallow
cared about the spring snow
And I watched
wishing you were alive, and with me
feeling your presence and your love
though I can touch you no more

The morning glory has unfolded
and the bird has much to say
Its footprints quickly danced
upon the newly fallen snow

Gazing at your photo, mementos and space
I recall you unfolding like the flower
and your life so like
the footprints of the bird
as time records your brief alighting
And you returned on high
to your endless journey

Yes
Your heart has walked on this lifetime
leaving its fleeting impressions
and like the morning glory you opened your
heart,
and mine,
and I honor the glory
of this mourning

Timelessness

The days whisper
of timelessness
yet you
worry
about time

Boundaries shout
they are too tight
until you must muffle your ears

Yes
work
and play
and rest

The days whisper
The time shouts

And your inner voice
knows

Your Happiness

Your
happiness
now
depends
on
your life
not
on
his death

The Beginning